CW00524576

WOUNDED ANGELS

MURRAY BODO

Wounded Angels

Blissfool Books

www.blissfool.co.uk

First published in 2009
by Blissfool Books
www.blissfool.co.uk

Printed in Great Britain by the MPG Books Group, Bodmin and King's Lynn

All rights reserved
© Murray Bodo 2009

The right of Murray Bodo to be identified as author of this work has been
asserted in accordance with Section 77 of the Copyright, Designs and
Patents Act 1988

This book is sold subject to the condition that it shall not, by way of trade
or otherwise, be lent, resold, hired out or otherwise circulated without the
publisher's prior consent in any form of binding or cover other than that in
which it is published and without a similar condition including this condition
being imposed on the subsequent purchaser

A CIP record for this book is available from the British Library

ISBN 978-0-9562372-0-0

Cover art: *Wounded Angel* (1903) by Hugo Simberg,
courtesy of the Ateneum Art Museum, Helsinki,
from photograph by Hannu Aaltonen
courtesy of the Central Art Archives

Cover design by Stephen King
Typeset by Jason Weaver

Mixed Sources
Product group from well-managed
forests, controlled sources and
recycled wood or fiber
www.fsc.org Cert no. TT-COC-002303
© 1996 Forest Stewardship Council
FSC

To Pat Mora and Vern Scarborough
in gratitude for your friendship and encouragement

*La belleza no es privilegio de unos cuantos nombres
ilustres.   Sería muy raro que este libro no atesorara
una sola linea secreta, digna de acompañarte hasta el fin.*
                              – Jorge Luis Borges

CONTENTS

Foreword by Herbert Lomas   x

Wounded Angel   3

i boy with junkyard dodge   5

Junkyard Dodge   7
Album   9
The Delmar Hotel: Gallup, New Mexico, 1947   11
The Wayward Wind   12
Shiprock, New Mexico   13
1945   14
Childhood Rug   15
The Southwest Chief   16
How Poems Begin   19
The Old Sporting Goods Store When He Was Twelve   21
Dad's Rifle   23
Gun Cleaning   24
Francis Bacon's, "Three Studies for a Crucifixion"   27
1948   28

ii tree with birds   29

Words that Fly   31
Storm-Petrel   32
A London Supper   34
Letter from Valentines Park, Ilford   35
Holy Relics   37
Watching Stones   38
Lady Pica   39
tree with birds   41

St. Francis and the Angel   43
St. Francis in Autumn   44
The Trees of San Damiano   45
Writing in Assisi   46
Righteous Gentile of Assisi   47
Music and Memory   48

iii jar with shells   **49**

After-Images   51
Triolet of the Dogwood   52
Daffodils   53
Roses   54
Seed   55
River at 70   56
Sea Turtles   57
Gull   58
Glass   59
Dream House   60
Jar with Shells   62

iv wounded angels   **63**

Wounded Angel 2   *65*

Hit and Run   66
A Hard Floor Ghazal   67
Nonno   69
Leaven   70
Crown of Thorns   71
Christmas, Inner City   73
homeless shelter   74

Sunday with Julian   75
Living Food   78
oasis   79
Men Riding the Rails, 1930   80
Wordsmith   81
Ulysses   83
Two Snapshots   85
Mysteries with Bells   86

v ending with beginning   **87**

Wounded Angel 3   *89*

Aristotle in Africa   90
Asylum City   91
Carol in a Climate of War   92
Hope   94
Passover   95
Cease Fire   96
After the War   97
Corpus Christi   98
parable   99
tsunami   100
Night Shift   101
transfigured signs   102
ending with beginning   103

Notes   109

Acknowledgements   111

Other Publications by Murray Bodo   113

Foreword

I met Murray Bodo in Assisi thirty-five years ago, and a year hasn't gone by since then without our managing to spend some time together, though he lives in Cincinnati inner city, and I by the English North Sea.

We were both staying at a little hostelry run by four Franciscan nuns, and he was writing his first book, *Francis, the Journey and the Dream*, a continuing classic that's sold over 200,000 copies and been translated into nine languages. He 'was' a Franciscan, and I 'was' a university lecturer, but we encountered each other as poets, and friends, and that is how it's been ever since.

'As poets'? What do I mean? Well, people who put words together, of course, and we've talked long and passionately about that and helped each other. But poems are about experience: they derive from what's undergone and felt, and their words create virtual experience – encouraging readers to create imaginative experience of their own.

Father Murray's been on a quest for the face of God since childhood, and there's no doubt about the force of that vocation, as well as the vocation of poet; and some of the experiences his quest has brought him have been formidable. He's always wanted to be a priest. Even at the age of eleven, with a muslin chasuble blowing in the wind, he invited seven kneeling children, boys and girls, Anglos and Mexicans, to come up for the adoration of the cross. But those romantic aspirations were followed by a hard school.

The son of a tough World War II marine, who was a trade

union leader and expert fly-fisherman and hunter, he's experienced the world in many guises: protesting against war with his friend Denise Levertov, the activist poet, counselling, helping and ministering to the poor where he and his brothers live, earning the Friary's living as the others do – he as a college Professor of English – conducting pilgrim groups round the Franciscan shrines in Italy, leading retreats, and making everyone he meets want to appoint him as their spiritual adviser. Laughing, joking, loving, still-more-than-half-Italian Dr. Bodo, author of so many spiritual classics, is the most human holy man you could ever meet, and the most fun.

But one must not overlook that he went through eight years of the dark night as soon as he had dedicated himself. He has movingly described in prose how he had to learn that books and asceticism were not going to give him the gift of grace. He had to be a human being as well as a priest, to know physically as well as intellectually that Christianity is a religion of *incarnation* in the flesh.

The poems are aware of how, simply by living, we hurt our fellow creatures:

> *The sudden shock*
> *seeing the squirrel*
> *in his rear-view mirror*
> *sealed to the road*
> *by his passing –*
> *another casualty*
> *behind him. (p. 66)*

And, more: how, by living in the collaterally murderous

mammon-driven consumerism we've inherited and continue to create, we're complicit. Personally, this is how I'd define original sin: 'the fathers have eaten sour grapes, and the children's teeth are set on edge', though Jeremiah was forbidden to use this saying again. I don't know what Murray would say, but I think he'd be in line with it. One of his fiercest poems is the story of his father finally striking the chin of the stepmother who'd constantly beaten him and leaving with his rifle at thirteen, never to return: 'When I was seven you taught me care / of the guns that would take care of me.' (p. 23) Yet Murray has turned from the guns. What is truth? as Pilate asked. 'Truth is a wounded angel / blind-folded so she can't see / what happened to her...' (p.3)

> *... we cart her home to show*
> *what someone else did to her... (p.3)*

Even our compassion is suspect.

What are the angels? They are many things or beings. For St Francis there were two angels: 'The lute angel... who played for him / afraid, alone / his eyes bleeding'; and the angel whose compassion for Christ wounded St Francis with the stigmata... – 'the two angels melding / into a Canticle of / God's wounding love'. (p. 43) He has felt Francis's wounds too.

This is the hurt centre of the book, but it makes possible the strength. The book opens with dreams – the happy dreams of boys, and the backward dreams of old men, remembering. There are adventures with Navajo Indians, memories of father fly-fishing, literally and imaginatively. There's a whole lifetime in this book – really several lifetimes; and Beauty, one of the three great Platonic attributes of God, along with Goodness and Truth.

How beautiful are roses
growing apart, not touching,
waiting for winged lips to drop
dust of another's embrace
between their virgin petals,   (p.54)

Now that he's seventy he knows that every afternoon could be the last afternoon.

It's when you realize this
could be the last afternoon
by the river, that the boy
in the red shirt skipping rocks
is still you seventy years
and thousands of miles ago next
to the rushing Pine River
watching Dad in hip boots wade
into the swirling Rainbows...   (p.56)

It's then that you realise the words you've fished for will run on like the river itself, for someone else to fish in.

Herbert Lomas (Aldeburgh)

wounded angels

Wounded Angel

After the painting by Hugo Simberg

Truth is a wounded angel
blindfolded so she can't see
what happened to her, so we
can't see her eyes illumine
what we're carrying inside:
how we're the very ones who
wounded her, how angel wings
drag our guilty hearts through dirt
as we cart her home to show
what someone else did to her.

3

i   boy with junkyard dodge

Junkyard Dodge

1

Opening its doors, he enters
the film he's come there to replay.
He sits behind the steering wheel
with Errol Flynn beside him.
Wind and wave buffet their ship
struggling to the foundering sloop
they'll save.
              He puffs a black cigar,
pretends he's not turning green.

Now, turning white, he
pretends it's not age
but adventure that waves
good-bye to land-locked
classrooms and chalk boards
to sail the junkyard Dodge.

2

Wind and rust and memory:
wind erratic, violent, driving sand
under the door of the glassed-in porch,
through cracks of wailing windows,
the little boy bundled beneath
woolen blankets, his radio propped

on the sill of the looming house
that tows his porch; the bed's iron
frame creaks like the wrecked and rusted
Dodge in the junkyard where he sneaks
away to find his dream ship and sail
far from the house of adults that hovers
above his bobbing dinghy.

Though furious wind threatens
the Dodge's ripping sails,
the boy feels safer there,
sitting on the bare springs
where upholstery used to be –
safer because no one knows he's
there in the serious playhouse
the man's sailing back to.

Will the old ships still anchor there
and childhood's doors still let
upon a magical Hollywood set

                                     or just

a scuppered wreck of whistling rust.

Album

Who's this child in the wicker chair
seven months old, 1938?
The man has no memory of the boy
on the tricycle, in the backyard
with the chickens; on the horse,
on the sled, in the high snow
with pots and pans around him.

Or in fishing photos at two years
of age, sitting sullenly on the grass,
Dad's Rainbow trout fanned out
like a deck of cards; or standing
next to a string of twenty trout
stretched like drying clothes.

At three he's wearing overalls or
Levi's with cowboy boots and hat,
sitting on a horse with his cousin;
behind the wheel of a junker car,
the caption: Ridges Basin, Colorado.
In sissy sailor suit or white pantsuit,
McGaffey Lake near, Gallup, 1941.

What to make of photos that are
supposed to be us and are at times
prophetic, glimpses of more than

the contours of the physical shape
we cut in the air around us: A half-
light displaces what is opaque for
the brief second the shutter clicks.
And there we were, and are, in
photo graphein: writing in light
who we were, till there's no one
to see; no images, no light.

The Delmar Hotel: Gallup, New Mexico, 1947

In the dream he's ten-years-old
watching Navajo women
selling turquoise jewelry
against the muraled wall
of Gallup's Delmar Hotel.

The mural begins to move,
a huge galleon bearing down
on the scared women who sink
in a squall of drowning words:
"Indian squaw, drunk, go back
to your own reservation."

He tries to swim out to them.
His arms, weighted with water,
won't lift, and he can't silence
the deafening words, or hail
the ship, its prow about to ram
the women reaching out to him.

The Wayward Wind

The first climb and curve of
the road into the Navajo Nation
was Shanty Meyers' trading post.

A silent, windswept bungalow,
there were seldom wagons or cars
parked where dark windows eyed

a boy in a Chevrolet, wide-eyed
for Shanty to step outside, wave
him by, point to adventures

a hill beyond what he could see.
Instead they sped by, the road as
usual as Shanty's empty porch.

Today Shanty's gone but not his
trading post or memories of
car and boy who later sped away

from a past the man now recalls:
a boy's dream of a place far away
that now brings him back where

Tex Ritter's voice used to moan
on radio, "The Wayward Wind"
that fooled with its wandering ways.

Shiprock, New Mexico

Lean horses wound the horizon.
Sand hills smolder in the mind.

He turns on the car radio.
Navajo Chant: Fire catches.
Suddenly, he's a boy: Horses
lift to a steady drum beat and
hills puff into clouds of sage.

No water falls from the sky,
but winged horses and floating
sand hills flow through a dry
brain thirsting for images:

Dawn Boy sings a horizon
where Ulysses' ship
lies hard aground,
and an ancient sea
needs only a boy
crossing the Navajo Nation
in a Chevy's back seat
dreaming the books he's read.

1945

He takes it to school for recess.
They grab the cords
and its great belly fills,

almost lifting them skywards as they
hold on for dear life, somehow
keeping the chute from flitting off.

It's the third grade boys' best
war performance to date:
they're the talk of the school.

This Japanese silk from Saipan
is Dad to Mother for dresses,
and Mother hums out her silk dresses.

But they're pale beside boys
torn between earth and sky, wanting
and not wanting to be lifted off

to war before their time,
or anyway
not before recess is over.

Childhood Rug

The lopsided Yeibichei dolls
in the Navajo rug on the wall

shrink from left to right and shrug,
"We're a perfect boy-child's rug."

They're over eighty now, each year
their imperfections more dear,

like old scars and bruises,
or the memory of what one loses.

Some say they trace an ugly track.
Square-headed Yei laugh back,

talk a walk in beauty apart
from proud and merely human art.

Some say the rug's just fit for saddles.
Fierce little Yei shake their rattles.

Some say the stick Yei look funny
the way they go from fat to skinny!

"Like you," they chant, "who age
and rattle and dry up like sage."

Like childhood's crayon pictures
they puzzle grownup tricksters.

The Southwest Chief

1

Training to Dad's funeral,
he enters the diner of the Southwest Chief.
When the maitre d' asks, "How many?"
and he says, "One," everything comes down.
He returns to his room and looks into the dark.
A full moon stares in on him staring back:
his own pupil, detached, floats in black night
follows him until they enter the hole called
Raton Pass. It reappears when they emerge,
a face etched in grey on the white moon
become his pupil leading him who once held it
secure in its own socket, thinking the eye
was not like one's face that changes
in the mirror as the eye does not, except
to grey a bit like the etchings on the moon
like hills and valleys when you see them on TV,
that other eye that looks back at you with news
from the moon, but this time from an astronaut's eye
or the camera that follows him about the moon
alone with heavy shoes that keep him from sliding
into space the way his eye did when he was asked
how many are you and his eye became the moon.

2

Does fondness for grey
go back to childhood's house on Fifth Street,
grey stucco, grey picket fence? And grey
with an "e" instead of an "a"?
What to make of that, "e" being British
and "a" American.
Or does spelling have more to do
with the feel of the word than how it's spelled
in what country?
"E" is right for that grey house on Fifth Street,
its fence, and the color of the faded images
I have of mother and dad and me
standing there in front of the rented house.
The picket fence keeps nothing but beans
and a few dahlias; it keeps the house
from dwarfing the picture of us standing there,
tryptich greyer now that Mother's gone
and Dad, and I am left an only child thinking
there should be more in the picture that can
never be anything but three with its
"e's" like the "e" in grey and the "e" in me
turned in upon itself, but not whole
like an "o," say, or four, the multiple of two,
or the moon still tracking me
farther now behind the train
where I take out the album I carry

to look at grey pictures of three
like the moon, the train, and me.

How Poems Begin

Dad fishes the Animas River
Durango, Colorado.
He's a small boy watching,
not knowing Dad's fishing for souls,

"Animas," in Spanish. He wades in,
casts, brings up Rainbow trout. But
now years later, the man sees souls
rising to the surface: his mother,

Nonna, and all his father's fishing
buddies, swimming just under
the surface of the river.
They wait for Dad to reel them toward

shore so the man can net them, place them
tenderly in his creel of
memories: Dad fishing, his
carefully tied flies fooling fish,

Mother baking, frying fish on stoves
fed by coal Dad mined in Nonna's
Durango; then the move to Gallup
where stories punctuate his boyhood:
Bruno Casna, drowned in the lake
at Blue Water, his dying-while-fishing
told over and over by Dad's buddies,

stories that keep the man too lost now
in reverie to try and snare real trout,
so beautiful as they swim in and out
of Dad's discarded fishing net.

The Old Sporting Goods Store When He Was Twelve

Les Leonesio, Lesio
"Bullshitta," his mother called him,
plunks down a hundred dollar bill,
says he'll shoot a deer through the eye

at a hundred yards. No one bites.
Undeterred, he repeats his dare.
Behind the kerosene stove the boy
sits wide-eyed, believes Les'll do it.

W.E. McNellis tells the boy
Browning guns were made by Fabrique
Nationale in Belgium. His
first French words and meeting with Mac.

"Hello, Gallup Sporting Goods Store."
"Well, I'll be damned; that's the number
I called. Is my little bastard
of a husband there?" "Yes, ma'am." "Well,
you tell him to get his ass on home."

Later he learns to handle her calls:
Lie and act dumb so Bonita
can stay and tell stories the boy
believes happened like he says.

Lesio, McNellis, Bonita.
Am I the only one who hears
you talking by the kerosene
stove? Gone so many years and none
but me to remember, to tell how
you kept a boy transfixed with lore,
most of it lies the way poems
lie to make us remember words.

Dad's Rifle

You took it with you to school, you said,
because you were seven already,

had to make your way — penny a tail
for prairie dogs shot to and from school.

Your second-grade teacher had agreed
to let you bring the gun, unloaded,

if you left it inside the back door
and saddled her horse after school.

At noon she'd let you take the rifle
a half hour to check your muskrat traps.

Once she tried to take the gun away,
but you left school, and she relented.

How could she have known your stepmother
was the only one you held in its sights,

she who beat you after school, locked you
in the closet till your dad came home?

At thirteen you punched her in the jaw,
took the rifle, and never returned.

When I was seven you taught me care
of the guns that would take care of me.

Gun Cleaning

I'm sitting on the floor, leaning
against mother's cedar chest,
cleaning your guns. I'm trying
to remember how, as best I can.
I'm using gun oil and old
ratty underwear and military
lubricant. I'm trying to remember,
even now, so many fathers after
you taught me how to do
what Father St. Francis undid.

I want to make the barrel shine again,
hold the warm light of the oiled stock,
forget the 270's blue flash that dropped
deer and elk, the Savage 12-gauge's
kick into my small shoulder
that drilled bb's into quail and cottontail,
pheasant and duck.

How beautiful these weapons,
how graceful the lines, how lethal
the fire of exploding powder
shooting sleek hot metal
from their round haloed barrels.

Darkness then, and death.

Was that what I learned as a boy?
Then why was there such light,
standing there beside you,
safe in your tough knowledge,
your code that tracked wounded game
to "put them out of their misery,"
inflicted by the same code that looked
like light to the boy feeling safe
beside his father, holding the guns
that meant we were or were becoming
men.
                    Arthritic, my hand
tries to grip the stock, pull the trigger
without wincing.
                    Just holding
the unloaded gun, hurts.
                              I still love
the feel of the wood, the dangerous
trigger, despite the pain in my hands,
but I wince at the images:
innocent, panicked eyes,
the sudden thump and splatter
of blood, the cries, the twitching,
the rigid silence.

                    This beautiful object
unmans me. Once it made me a man,
you said.

I put the half-cleaned guns in their proper cases.
I shove them under your and mother's bed
where they lie dark and silent and harmless
until I find their cool seduction again
and hesitate...

Dad, it's you I love –
if you're reading these lines.
Tell me again so I understand:
how the hunter loves animals,
how he's close to the land,
how eating is communion
with what died at your hand.

Francis Bacon's, "Three Studies for a Crucifixion"

I just painted the color of butcher stalls I saw as a boy at
Harrod's with my mother.
                                        – Francis Bacon

They're playing hide-and-seek,
Mother and he, running
under the slap of laundered sheets –
blind to Dad's fly line drying
across the hanging wash.

The hook dangles and rips
Mother's ear lobe: *Naked sides of beef*
appear, deer, rabbits nailed open
for gutting – and slapping trout,
gills exhaling blood.

He tries to stop the images now, but
they run and run like paint:
He's in Hog Johnson's
slaughterhouse, and he's four,
unable to stop the stench of blood.

It pours onto the floor where he stands
in red and purple puddles. Whatever
the painter saw he saw, feet
fixed to the slaughterhouse floor,
the barbed hook hanging.

1948

Some Sunday morning we'll walk down the aisle,
Some Sunday morning you'll be wearing a smile.

The boy didn't remember
the movie, only two lines
of a song, and he and mother
in the intimate dark.
He sees his mother happy:
she walks down the movie aisle
to the wedding lighting the screen.

The man sees the boy
walking mother down the aisle
to give her away. At the sanctuary
she doesn't stop but ascends
to the altar where she embraces
the monstrance: it becomes a dahlia
like those she stands among, a young girl
in the photo on his desk. She smiles
dressed in gay formality, ready
to walk into her future singing:

Some Sunday morning . . .

ii tree with birds

Words that Fly

Do words take us further
than we could go without them?
Are words themselves what
we must trust the way we
trusted those who took us
by the hand, put us on those
rides that looked scary
to our small selves alone?
And didn't we learn
to ride roller coasters, think
there wasn't anything
we couldn't do? That is,
until there was no one
to hold our hand. Alone,
we were afraid to board
the rides and were left
behind the way we are now
by words we're afraid
to befriend all alone
–until we do make tryst,
hold hands with "turbulence,"
"falling," and "terrorist."

31

Storm-Petrel

As they fly...they pat the water alternately with their Feet,
as if they walkt upon it; tho' still upon the Wing. And from
thence the Seamen gave them the name of Petrels, in allusion
to St. Peter's walking upon the Lake of Gennesareth.
                        – W. Dampier Voyage III, I. 97

Always and on all sides water,
yet more, heavy weather.

Clouds low and slow fog thick
fog horn's blow and spray of quick

souls lifting from waves, their wet wings
spent myth that quivers and flings

brief resurrections, mere sea horses –
Pegasus versus forces

weighted with dark gravity,
whose fathoms threaten buoyancy.

Then tossed wings: a kittiwake,
frantic in the storm-ship's wake

pats its feet on the whipping waves,
though on wing, and braves

the merciless wind landward,
this Storm-Petrel: for him who heard

the word on Galilee's sea where
he flailed sinking, gasping for air.

A London Supper

Off Victoria Street in Westminster
Cathedral Square homeless evangelists
lay like apostles at a McDonald's
Passover meal. Apocalyptic John
leaned on his elbow and prophesied
to the sky, while the other three listened
rapt, as if he spoke to them. That ecstatic
wine-induced gospel shamed my meditation.

St. Francis, would have joined
their circle, found among the down and out
dispossessed Divinity, instead of
tongues I refused because I did not hear
my own. Or was it simply fear that I
might end up preaching to the empty sky?

Letter from Valentines Park, Ilford

In memory of Denise Levertov

The park off Cranbrook Road
is flower beds and bird song,
a bench with solitary figure.

Your once mesmerizing stream's
now clogged with candy wrappers,
the stagnant water a goo of leaves.

The fountain's still, its surface
an algae raft where klutzy
mud-hen chicks walk on water.

A duck and eight ducklings slip
bravely on slime-slick fountain steps,
once a watery merry-go-round.

On the sandy wishing well's bed
a dull penny's dusted with ashes
from which no phoenix rises.

Still, the gardens are cherished:
careful beds of dahlias, geraniums,
gazantia, ageratum, mums,

Silver Dust, and Busy Lizzie,
your beloved English impatiens,
whose fierce colors startle the eye.

A 300-year-old Mulberry's fenced in
to protect it from children like you
who *will* clamber over its branches.

Only a trickle of water resolves its way
through pop bottles and fast-food
containers toward the Roding River.

The late train leaves before I can follow
your doll carriage down York Road,
Jean Rankin in tow, to Wanstead Park,

its "basic poetry" only imagined
in the receding girls with carriage
entering the unseen woods.

Holy Relics

Silent the tombs where bone-specimens
lie for inspection –
relics no different to the eye than
those of kings and queens
or the anonymous peasant whose tomb
was field or forest.

Where are the souls that quickened us
and brought us here – pilgrims
seeking more than an arrangement of bones?

Yet, the air
does sing with their signature.
Sometimes everywhere.

Watching Stones

Heavy as fatted cattle
Assisi heat lumbers through
the piazza, leaderless.

A hot sirocco summons
dull onlookers who stumble
on burning cobblestones.

Eyes glaze over facades that
pulse their own cryptic message:
Don't look at us, keep walking.

We'll open when you cool off,
slow down for us to watch you.

Lady Pica

Francis, dear one
the empty rooms cry out for you
and under the chimney's hood
the hearth fire burns untended
I sit in an upright chair

It is months now – your father
fusses with palfreys and war horses
while I shun linens and wool dresses
trimmed and lined with fur

And no one sees
I sit by the window
I hear rumors
I stay inside
I sit in an upright chair

There is no song here
except for the birds I hear
through the window's oiled parchment
The days are long

Your father roars
at the dogs and servants
and we seldom sit by the fire
The night frightens our sleep

Francesco, my son
what have I done?
Tell me how it is with you
knock at the silent door
I wait in an upright chair

They say you're now a leper –
Dear one, what has become of you?
Your father and I lie abed
stare at the ceiling's wooden beams

Your dog whines mornings
He watches the door
He does not eat
I pat his matted coat

I give you to God, my son
I wait for death
The bells toll under the house
The wind laughs in the eaves
I sit in an upright chair

tree with birds

st francis saw the kingdom
sheltering the birds

its branches twisted
sideways

but reaching
toward the sky

he told the birds
be thankful

for the shade
and many perches

of the twisted
earthly kingdom

and they sat
and listened

and said amen
and flew

to the four branches
of the earth

perching on the kingdom
sitting in its shade

tree growing sideways
reaching for the sky

St. Francis and the Angel

Which angel, though,
the lute angel of Rieti
who played for him
afraid, alone
his eyes bleeding?

Or the angel of La Verna
Seraph whose wings
covered the man
crucified
whose suffering
burned Francis' heart
till wounds broke
through his own body?

He rose then broken
like a note
from a wounded lute,
the two angels melding
into a Canticle of
God's wounding love.

St. Francis in Autumn

This year's olives are small, spare.
Late September swallows tear

through gray morning mist silent
as in early August their strident

cries caught fire in smoldering dawn.
Now sparrows hop singly, hangers on

from summer flocks dwindled to twos
or threes in the weather's moods.

A dove in dingy ballerina white
struts rimed roofs, not taking flight.

Year by year fall landscapes change
little; the same different birds range

for food on the bare streets of Assisi
or fly south in the cold broth, uneasy.

The Trees of San Damiano

St. Clare hears of the death of Francis

The same olive trees still grow
below the city gate on the hill
that slopes to San Damiano.

Old, their gnarled fingers twist
upward to the sun, like my heart
reaching for that sunlit tryst:

you and Philip, me and my friend,
Bona, beneath the silvered leaves that
trembled after the hot sirocco's end.

I look at the gate we saw was closed
to us and what we talked of, beyond
their vision, those who had supposed

us outside what prelates would allow
though we were in the poor God's Body
nailed to the tree that supports me now.

Writing in Assisi

Even now
nearing seventy,
there is the daily making:
pen against paper,
curling letters into words
solid and smooth as the wood
of the carver whose cave-like studio
I pass each morning
on my way for cappuccino and brioche.
He keeps his mallet and chisel
warm against the chipping wood
to feed his family. But I suspect
he chips away every day,
mallet to chisel to wood,
to surprise himself
with something more than food.

Righteous Gentile of Assisi

Don Aldo Brunacci (1914-2007)

Pigeons sleep on the railings
of windows opposite mine.

Echoes pulsate from the stones
where I last saw Don Aldo,

a frail 92, his cane
gently tapping away from me

toward the Piazza del Comune
at the end of Via San Paolo.

I watched him walking, it seemed,
forever, and the piazza – like

the Jewish refugees he sheltered
and saved from harm – kept

receding from his determined will.
I see him walking still,

his short shuffle out of step
among friends and passersby.

Music and Memory

So here it is, the end of summer
and the accordion's playing
strains of "Saints Go Marching In,"
even here in Italy, the mountains
of Rieti listening in the cool night.
In three days I'll rise
into the clear sky, the Boeing
747 like a huge prehistoric
dinosaur lifting off the ground.
"Oh Susanna" filters through
my listening window, and I'm
back in Bardstown, Kentucky
watching *The Stephen Foster Story*.

The notes stir the still
unfigured future into being
and hope dances to that chord
common in us, deep with longing
for finding what we did not know
was lost until the melody began,
and a forgotten folk tune
floats the heart in air.

Who is it in me that knows
it's more than summer ending?
Can I say who it is? Age perhaps,
or a stage, or more accurately a way
of listening that is more than memory.

iii   jar with shells

After-Images

He keeps seeing things after he's passed them.
It comes from riding the train, seat backwards.
There's no prescience that way, only surprises.
Sometimes he wishes he'd seen what's coming,
but then, watching it recede is like the memory
of a never realized future that worrying over
wouldn't have changed now that it's passed.

The train that lashes past could have threatened,
they might've collided head on;
but now it's gone.
                          He likes sitting seat backward.

Triolet of the Dogwood

God sings in the dwarf dogwood:
small white mouths open in vowels
that sing but don't sound.

God sings where winter's sound
was the soft hiss of dogwood,
sibilants without vowels.

A circle of four-petaled vowels,
blossoms of round sound:
God sings in the baby dogwood.

Sound of dogwood, breathless vowels.

Daffodils

He's looking at the daffodils
she gave him, their three faces
frontal, in profile and coyly
oblique. Two white and one yellow,
they are growing from the mouth
of the brown beer bottle where
she planted them.

He's been looking at them
all morning on the windowsill that faces
his desk. The one in the middle, yellow,
lowest of the three, its mouth
open, tries to draw him into
the soft lime-colored center where
he'd no longer see the other daffodils

each profile a hint of mouth that faces
the yellow fuzz of curtain cleverly
drawn to give all three daffodils
room to turn away from where
he'd surely try to hold them.

Roses

How beautiful are roses
growing apart, not touching,
waiting for winged lips to drop
dust of another's embrace
between their virgin petals.

Seed

The wind blows,
the seed falls into the ground.
It's cold there, dark.
But something stirs within,
pushes on the seed's hard shell
until it breaks, and something soft
gropes through dirt-and-rock rungs
towards where it fell from.

It's blind but sees.
The ooze of seeds keeps giving,
exuding the soft, pliable shoot.
It grows longer, the seasons change.
Water softens the soil.
The sun waits.

River at 70

It's when you realize this
could be the last afternoon
by the river, that the boy
in the red shirt skimming rocks
is still you seventy years and
thousands of miles ago next
to the rushing Pine River
watching Dad in hip boots wade
into the swirling Rainbows.

It's when you look up from lines
of words and the boy is gone,
that you realize rivers,
fishing or skimming rocks, kept
words weighted like sinkers
or bobbing on the surface
of your memory – and now
what you see and remember
are the same words becoming

the river, the boy, and you.
The words, like the river, run
in syllables someone else will
fish in when you reel in your
line the last late afternoon.
It's then that you linger
longer by any shore of
river, lake, stream or stanza.

Sea Turtles

In the dark night's rake – waves
trembling against the shore –

they surface from their sleek world
to stumble like drunken sailors

up rough cusps of sand.
Their fins struggle to scoop out

nests to drop their eggs
in ancient patterns.

Spent, they grope and struggle,
plop back into the sea.

Though their element is water,
the turtles drop life in sand.

Over head, sleek-shelled jets
streak in their element,

drop clumsy bombs on land.

Gull

in memory of Brother John Schreck, OFM

Out walking the beach tonight
my flashlight's beam lit upon
some white indenting the sand,
a large lump of stilled feathers.

Yesterday he stood there almost
motionless as large earth movers
rumbled past hauling away sand
piled high where the beach was

before the hurricanes. The gull
seemed old, confused, resigned
to everything being rearranged
and he too spent to fly away.

I walked past twice, but like
the children playing, didn't stop
until that flash of white, my light
finding the still feathered body.

Death and something else chilled:
your silent cry, your face wan
on white sheets, and the swift
feet that passed by unaware.

Glass

Surf-spun glass
    shimmers wingless
        in the morning light.

Flung from the sea,
    it cobbles the beach
        with the depths' dark sheen.

Wrung snug in the palm,
    brown shards warm
        as you carry them home

where sun on window sills
    dulls what sand and waves
        tumbled to luminescence.

Dream House

The waves I love
are eating the cliff
where I live
in the white cottage.

I hear
underneath the house
the waves I see
through the porch window.

You'd think
the land stopped them,
the way they bounce back
from the rocks
the house is built upon.

But I hear them
running under me
like the hurts we had
as children
and wonder now
where they've gone.
They're somewhere inside
beating against the brain,
seeping into the passages,
eating the barriers
we live behind.

We float
in their water
and imagine
we're just flesh.

The white cottage
that fronts the sea
is all a dream,
its fences
unable to keep out
what's already inside.

Jar with Shells

Rinsed with salt water,
the shell shines.
Dry, its luster dulls
to souvenir,
a shell like other
vague memories
scrabbling fingers
try to retrieve
from the glass jar.

iv   wounded angels

Wounded Angel 2

That impulse to bring home the body
as if we are helping mercifully
grateful the victim hasn't eyes to show
we were complicit in the wounding,
the slaughter. Caring for the bodies,
we manage to canonize our own
murderous hearts, brave in showing
others our compassion, intent on
blinding the eyes that saw what we deny.

Hit and Run

The sudden shock
seeing the squirrel
in his rear-view mirror
sealed to the road
by his passing –
another casualty
behind him.

A Hard Floor Ghazal

It's hard for the father to watch the boy,
face down on the investiture floor,

receive his new Franciscan name
and rise a stranger on a different shore.

To the doubtful father the rite's harder
than the hard unyielding floor.

When he sees there's no more to say,
he leaves his son at the novitiate door,

goes home with the boy's mother
and closes the sporting goods store

where the boy read books between
customers on the fire arms floor.

He takes his wife and rifle, flees
to the mountains to camp and pour

his grief into hunting. He comes home,
lives his life, and sees another floor —

the priesthood — receive his prostrate son.
He says the church lays a hard floor.

When his mother dies, the son asks
the father, can they go fishing once more.

They cast bait and know she prayed
they'd fish and talk as before.

When the father dies, the son kneels
at the casket on the church's marble floor.

Nonno

I never knew Nonno, mother's father;
he died of black lung before I was born.
All I have is a photo and two quotes
of his about Church and eternity:
"I went to church enough in Italy."
And "You don't remember the way it was
before you were born, do you? Well, you won't
remember things after you're dead either."

In the photograph two children, mother
and my uncle, stand awkward and forlorn
beside Nonna's seated grace. Behind her
standing apart, is Nonno: short and bald
and mustache heavy, he looks like he
can't remember where he's come from or where
he's going or why they're all still posing.

Leaven

for my uncle, Aldo Bonan

In the photo you wear your baker's cap
Sinatra style – a jaunty memory –
but your hands rest heavy on stainless steel
like dough beneath moistened linen towels.
By night you'd stand and stack ovens with bread
while I slept soundly in a comfortable bed.
And when I rose at 6am for Mass,
stacked loaves lay on tables floured
white as altar cloths and priestly albs.
Now my hands, heavy at your Requiem,
lift the light unleavened bread. I bow,
leaven the flat bread with words: "This is
my Body which is given up for you."
Christ becomes your rising in my hands.

Crown of Thorns

in memory of Fr. Leander Blumlein, OFM

Good Friday, transplanting
Crown of Thorns shrubs,
I remember how your
flower beds ordered
the college courtyard.

English teacher, director
of plays, you transplanted
young clerics to gardens
of culture and literature:
Bernanos, Mauriac, & Bloy
Hopkins, Eliot, & Waugh.

You planted texts
that would bear fruit
and taste bitter to you
when Vatican II
struck like a hoarfrost.
You felt we'd betrayed
the cultivated garden:

the vulgar weeds
of "hootenanny" Masses
for Plain Chant; improv
for the formal design
of the Latin liturgy.

These bushes prick soft skin,
their thorns almost expiation,
an offering ….
               I'd never
have dreamed of killing
a spiritual father, but
something akin happened
when we began to plant
and work new flower beds,
and you remained rooted
and wounded, a Crown of
Thorns choking your heart.

You died outdoors, running
through a dark wood wild.

Christmas, Inner City

It's the night before Christmas
And police patrol cars are
Keeping their slow watch by night.

A teenage mother cradles
Her baby against the cold.
The streets are silent and dark

When suddenly three angels
Break through the dark, their voices
High and sweet with "Silent Night,"

Their parents hovering near.
The young mother stops and listens,
The small angels sing bravely.

Suddenly light illumines
Our inner city lot where
All is still, patrol cars stop,

And God's a baby again.

homeless shelter

spilt soup spreads
on the bed

drips over the edge
to the floor

where angry
mops

slop up
her dream

of eating soup
in bed

Sunday with Julian

She consoles me as I meditate
before Mass – Julian of Norwich,
that is, who says, "We are clothed,
wrapped in the goodness of God."

And she consoles me after Mass,
when I drive home to the friary and
pass two prostitutes who are sitting
on folding chairs next to the curb
helping each other with make-up.

And that evening, too, when I go
to Frisch's for a Big Boy and fries
and a boy's talking to his girl friend
in the booth next to mine – talking
and talking – and his girl friend's
eyes say she just wants to hold him
and quiet him – and he keeps talking
and her eyes keep trying to say,
Let's leave.

      And when I leave, he's
still talking, "You know what I'm
saying?" and she's still trying to
subtly persuade him they should
leave and then I'm walking behind

a middle-aged man, a son helping
his older mother to the car and ahead
an older man's walking with his pregnant
teen-age wife and she's smiling as he
talks and eats an ice cream cone and I
think, the Mass still isn't over.

And as I get into the car, Julian's in
my thoughts again and I say to myself,
They're all clothed in the goodness
of God – and I'm about to drive away
when a prostitute, tattooed abundantly,
comes to my open window and asks,
"Do you have a lighter I could buy
from you?" and I say, "No, but I can
give you some matches" and she says,
"I don't do matches," and I'm wondering
is there a code here I'm not aware of? and
she says, "Hey, you're the guy who didn't
give me a ride earlier, aren't you?" and
of course I was and didn't, fearing what
it might look like, forgetting Julian, and
she says, "I said to myself, *Okay, I like
the jerk anyway*," and walks away.

And then I drive away and it's twilight
and I'm left with memories of this day
and I think, Yes, Julian, we are wrapped

in God's goodness, and yes, the Mass
begins when it ends. And when I get
home, I pick up Julian and she says,
"Mother Jesus leads us into his blessed
breast through his open side, and there
gives us a glimpse of the Godhead and
heavenly joy…" The Mass begins.

Living Food

The scent of you
comes first
then the vision.

The bathless stench
you leave on my car seat
the day I drive you
to the Gas and Electric.

The acrid smoke
from your dirty grill
in the alley
beneath my window.
The proferred stew
I can't eat.

Who was it said
you are living food?

oasis

John 8:1-12

they've trapped me
in the sand

they gather stones
to blame me

then he kneels and
scribbles in the sand

they leave me alone
with the man

my oasis
i drink his words

Men Riding the Rails, 1930

Tck-tck, tck-tck, tck-tck.
Wheels on rails turn, tck-tck:
hope making its steady
way to something better.

Not smoothly, but across
breaks where rails laid ahead
of leaving set the course
we rock toward like clumsy
beasts, appetites thumping
toward.

       Returning, we rattle
on empty, our hearts grind
on rough rails. The main line
ended at sidings, exits.

Wordsmith

Spare, aging African-American,
gray goatee and tenor voice,
sings as he shines my shoes –
Union Station, Chicago.

"Song and a shine,
that's good," I say.
"Thank you, sir. Your
kindness will be

obliterated."

He winks and signals
another to the padded
high chair that makes men
feel like children again,
their feet pampered through
tough, protective leather.

I've not had a shine for years,
though I've lived among
yet apart from those who
obliterate dirt and grime, keepers
of what keeps our feet.

Was that where I'd have kept him,
had not a word elevated

81

what stereotyping keeps at our feet,
like this wordsmith I'd not
have suspected, until shoes

sparked his song, and my words
snapped the rag of his wit
into a word that hit?

Ulysses

– After Cesare Pavese

Another embittered old man
who was too old to have a son. Oh,
they'd eye each other from time to time,
but a slap in the face fixed that.
The man would leave, return with the boy
clutching his shoulder, eyes down.
                    Now the old man sits
at the big window waiting for dark.
The street's deserted, no one is coming.

This morning the boy left. He'll return
tonight wearing a contemptuous sneer.
He won't let on if he's eaten or not.
No, sullen eyed, he'll go to bed
in silence, his boots sullied with mud.

                    After a month of rains
the morning was blue.

Through the cool window, a bitter scent
of leaves. It's dark, but the old man doesn't
budge. He's no longer sleepy at night,
though he'd love to sleep and forget, the way
he used to, coming home after a long walk,
shouting, boxing the air to keep warm.

The boy, who'll return shortly, is too big
for slapping. He's turning into a man.
Every day he's discovering things he's
not talking about to anyone.

There's nothing you can't see on the road if you
stand at the window. The boy roams
the road all day long. He's not looking
for women, not yet, and he's no longer
playing in mud. And though he still comes back,
he has a way of leaving that says, take one last
look, and don't try to stop me.

Two Snapshots

You stand there stripped of the boat you thought
you'd sail, the condominium's frail promise,
him who said, "I'll marry you," and didn't
when you lost the ovary and a slip
of the laser sliced nerves which the surgeon
still denied after months of chronic pain,
you being hysterical woman and therefore
dispensable as the rubber gloves dropped
cavalierly into a container
some cleaning woman empties.
A photo of a homeless woman is fixed
by magnets to your refrigerator
where you look furtively, afraid to see
yourself there: Broken health, no husband, no
home, no promise. Two men, both exuding
confidence, fidelity to their word,
strip you of the words they gave and leave you
mute as what their denials fail to say.

Mysteries with Bells

And then there are the mysteries
their singing and high-ringing bells.

We need to believe, so we do,
the singing mysteries with bells.

But the homeless man with dog
sings for a handout without bells.

The mysteries sing the fiver
and we believe something happened.

The song and the man with dog:
mysteries without bells or fuss.

The dog jumps, the man invites us
to the homeless ball without bells.

And then there are the mysteries,
their singing and high-ringing bells.

v   ending with beginning

Wounded Angel 3

Your cynical heart's a bandage.
I cannot see to help you.

Your doubt crippled my wings.
I let you carry me home,

an angelic caricature
that only you can cure.

Aristotle in Africa

He was reading Aristotle's *Poetics*.
I asked for his opinion. He thought
the story strong in its object of
imitation, the telling quite terse prose,
the manner ironic narrative.

The professor thought the dramatic
action was the President's, the action
off-stage insignificant to the tragedy.
I said we who escaped dared disagree,
located the tragedy at the university.

I told him 200 poisoned bayonets
had killed 100 sleeping students.
By 4 A.M. their bodies had disappeared,
the bloody stage was rinsed. He said,
Though sad, it's a splendid mimesis.

I don't hate him though I'm convinced
the Professor knew the students knew,
so the President killed them in bed.
The Professor dared not know he knew,
so he killed the real story instead.

Asylum City

Across from my balcony
rises offices of the UN High
Commission for Refugees.

Its high radio antenna sags,
weighted with birds seeking
roosts on its metal branches.

I count 288 windows –
there are more – on this side.
Nearby, asylum seekers roost

in what looks like windowless
double-decker gypsy trailers.
Geneva forbids them work.

And so they hover under
helpless windows that stare
blank as owls' eyes at noon.

They're given food stamps, bus
tickets, & cell phones they can
be tracked by, like banded birds.

Carol in a Climate of War

What music now
21 centuries after
Mary sang in our flesh,

"I am Your servant;
be fashioned in me."
Her words now vie

with words not hers
who opened her womb
to the Angel's word.

Frenetic flapping sings
of fabricated wings
trapped in human words

that refuse the invitation
to embody God's Word.
The powerful screech,

"Glory to us on high,
woe to those who won't
join us in war's chorus."

But Angels sing the antiphon,
"Kneel before the little Word
who's swaddled – wordless."

Baby purls, animal sounds,
silent Mary, Joseph nearby,
turn our war-cry to lullaby.

Hope

The mercury falls
              before the sun rises
white through black trees.

American bombs fall
              on Iraq
as justifying blather rises.

My heart sinks
              at this fall from grace
as sap rises towards spring.

St. Joseph's Feast
              falls today
as smoke rises over Bagdad.

Slaughter of the Innocents:
              laments rise
as women and children fall.

Though bodies fall like leaves,
              shoots rise,
improbable, from bomb-exhausted ground.

Passover

As though nothing has happened
they keep up appearances –
"Early Bird Special" Fridays,
after which, their evening stroll
to "work off" dinner, delay
going home to watch TV.
No one notices their masked
pain, their wooden pace since he
came home, a metal box from
Iraq. Their route is cyclic,
unvaried. The angel has
not passed over; they have no
child, just tired bodies and
minds not trying not to die.

Cease Fire

It's one of those afternoons
when you see the rain inching
upriver and the river's
half sun, half cloudy with rain.
You stand in the sun and smell
rain, and the rain starts falling
though you're pooled in sunlight.

A crow sits on the railing
of the porch you've ducked into
and a boat full of rain slides
into sunlight, and the smell
of rain lingers but briefly.
The crow flies onto the roof.
It's hot again and humid.

You look upriver for clouds
and a rain boat to take you home.

After the War

We look to our cemeteries.
Some are not yet destroyed, sold

or changed to something other.
What if they should dig up our dead

to make room for a shopping mall,
a freeway, a bingo hall?

We need to protect our relics
as ancients guarded their saints

lest rivals snatch the power
electric in their bones.

We won't forget who they were,
or the plot that marks what war does.

Corpus Christi

Two sand hill cranes walk the parking lot
next to Kentucky Fried Chicken, heads
high and alert for danger and food.

It's Thursday of Holy Week,
Christ offering himself as our food,
while we sit at the drive-in window

snug in air-conditioned comfort
watching the cranes' cautious approach
to us who could feed them or harm them.

Their hunger is courage, ours is numbed
response to what someone offers through
drive-in windows or death on a cross.

parable

i was looking
at the birds of the air

when hunters
shot them down

and i saw the lilies
die of too much cold

no one seemed
to be watching over

but birds still sing
lilies bloom

not foreseeing
not fretting

they die
a happy life

we live
a worried death

tsunami

beneath debris and stench
a hand

your hand withered
stretched forth

waiting for someone's
be healed

too late
jesus is gone

only the story's left
and we

afraid of his power

Night Shift

Rail cars drift,
try to connect.

They clack against
each other, back

and forth, their track
the mind's rail at

night when words
lie fast unheard

beneath dream cars
rattling apart.

Words wake – work to
hitch the distant cars.

transfigured signs

mt. 17

a column of cloud
hides the sun

Jesus shines
on Moses and Elijah

bright cloud's
shadow

surrounds Peter
James and John

cloud and shadow
somewhere's sun

speaking "my Beloved"
where now

only Jesus stands
touches humans

face down
on ground

opening to their
radiant bodies

ending with beginning

three poems for my mother

still life

kitchen bar with telephone –
not planes only and surfaces –

but textures:
you sitting there

answering the phone
the last time we talked

your voice still bright as
your pain was constant

and me sitting in the empty
house when you died

staring at the kitchen bar
waiting for the phone to ring

and months later
lifting the phone

hundreds of miles away
almost calling that number

that phone, that
voice, that kitchen bar

as far as you are near
as near as you are far

Sewing Box

I have the sewing box and pillow cases
you embroidered – having no children
to give them to. They comfort and hurt,
these flowered calligraphies, and the busy
sewing box I'd organize on visits home.

It's a memory chest, dream embroiderer,
and you light of foot, hurrying home
from drudgery at the Elite Laundry
to mend socks and hearts; later your step
finical, trying to side step pain, your sewing
labored – with little left for me to organize.

It's a sepulcher whose spools of thread,
buttons, thimbles, needles and pins,
are stilled, except for this my anniversary-
fussing with loose threads, drawing
them out straight, patting and checking
to see what's there, what's possibly
not there, these, can it be almost
twenty years of slow erasure?

This year I found a hidden drawer
not noticed before, a map of
home, avenues of nouns and static
verbs: Irontex Renew-a-Pocket,

25 cents a pair, no sewing, iron on!
And the felt needle-keeper cut-out
of a bonneted girl's silhouette I made
for you in fourth grade, whose black
bonneted head you trimmed in white
crocheted frill.

The Irontex envelope
contains the patches, two holy cards,
prayers to Our Lady and a pamphlet
entitled, "La Communione dei Fedeli."

Working Girl

I'm making my bed.
You live in my hands

your arthritis growing
in mine.

From my desk
you smile among dahlias

the photo faded
your bobbed hair tight

as a bud, your purse light
in hands not gnarled

as when I watched you
smooth my bed the last time.

Your scrapbook lies open:
A girl's elastic hand glues

pressed petals that rattle now
among the brittle pages.

Notes

p. 19: "Nonna" is the Italian word for grandmother.

p. 27: The quote from Francis Bacon is from an audio-guide at a Bacon exhibit at the Tate Museum, London. Of Bacon, John Berger has written, "In his art pain is being watched through a screen, like soiled linen being watched through the round window of a washing machine." (*The Shape of a Pocket*, p. 160)

p. 28: The second line does not appear in the Helen Forest and the Dick Haymes song, but the two lines together is how the child and then the man remembered them.

p. 32: The quote from the epigraph is from the Oxford English Dictionary.

p. 33: "basic poetry" is from a line in Denise Levertov's poem, "A Map of the Western Part of the County of Essex in England": "Wanstead drew me over and over into its basic poetry."

p. 69: "Nonno" is the Italian word for grandfather.

p. 83: "Ulysses" is a rendering of the poem, "Ulisse," from *Lavorare Stanca* by Cesare Pavese (1908-1950).

p. 106: "La Communione dei Fedeli" is the Italian for "The Communion of the Faithful."

Acknowledgements

I would like to thank Don Bogen and Herbert Lomas who read the manuscript in progress and offered invaluable suggestions; Richard Howard, poet and editor and mentor extraordinaire; my editor, Victoria Bennett and her husband Adam, who graciously took on this book to launch their new imprint, Blissfool Books. Also thanks to the following publications where some of the poems of this volume were first printed:

Waxwing: "Wounded Angel," "Wounded Angel 2," and "Wounded Angel 3"

Western Humanities Review: "Gun Cleaning," and "Francis Bacon's, 'Three   Studies for a Crucifixion'"

St. Anthony Messenger: "Oasis," and "Parable"

The Cord: "Writing in Assisi," "The Trees of San Damiano," "St. Francis in Autumn," "Lady Pica," and "tree with birds"

The Cincinnati Review: "Daffodils," and "Cease Fire"

Image: "Sewing Box"

The Cincinnati Review (Winter 2007 Issue): "Daffodils" and "Cease Fire,"

Western Humanities Review (Winter 2008 Issue):   "Francis Bacon's, 'Three Studies for a Crucifixion'"

Other Publications by Murray Bodo

Francis, the Journey and the Dream (1972)

Song of the Sparrow (1976, new revised edition 2008)

Clare, a Light in the Garden (1979, new, revised edition, 1992)

Sing Pilgrimage and Exile [Poems] (1980)

The Way of St. Francis (1984)

Through the Year with Francis of Assisi (1987)

Tales of St. Francis (1988)

The Almond Tree Speaks, New and Selected Writings:
1974-94 (1994)

A Retreat with Francis and Clare of Assisi
(with Susan Saint Sing) (1996)

Tales of an Endishodi: Father Berard Haile and the Navajos,
1900-1961 (1998)

The Threefold Way of St. Francis (2000)

Poetry as Prayer: Denise Levertov (2001)

Icarus in Assisi [Poems] (2002)

Poetry as Prayer: Francis of Assisi (2003)

Landscape of Prayer (2003)

The Earth Moves at Midnight [Poems] (2003)

The Place We Call Home: Spiritual Pilgrimage as a
Path to God (2004)

Mystics: Ten Who Show Us the Ways of God (2007)